K NOTES

Henry V

William Shakespeare

Notes by David Langston

Longman

YORK PRESS
322 Old Brompton Road, London SW5 9JH

ADDISON WESLEY LONGMAN LIMITED
Edinburgh Gate, Harlow,
Essex CM20 2JE, United Kingdom
Associated companies, branches and representatives throughout the world

First published 1998

ISBN 0–582–36829–4

Designed by Vicki Pacey, Trojan Horse, London
Illustrated by Judy Stevens
Phototypeset by Gem Graphics, Trenance, Mawgan Porth, Cornwall
Colour reproduction and film output by Spectrum Colour
Produced by Addison Wesley Longman China Limited, Hong Kong

CONTENTS

032538

PREFACE

York Notes are designed to give you a broader perspective on works of literature studied at GCSE and equivalent levels. We have carried out extensive research into the needs of the modern literature student prior to publishing this new edition. Our research showed that no existing series fully met students' requirements. Rather than present a single authoritative approach, we have provided alternative viewpoints, empowering students to reach their own interpretations of the text. York Notes provide a close examination of the work and include biographical and historical background, summaries, glossaries, analyses of characters, themes, structure and language, cultural connections and literary terms.

If you look at the Contents page you will see the structure for the series. However, there's no need to read from the beginning to the end as you would with a novel, play, poem or short story. Use the Notes in the way that suits you. Our aim is to help you with your understanding of the work, not to dictate how you should learn.

York Notes are written by English teachers and examiners, with an expert knowledge of the subject. They show you how to succeed in coursework and examination assignments, guiding you through the text and offering practical advice. Questions and comments will extend, test and reinforce your knowledge. Attractive colour design and illustrations improve clarity and understanding, making these Notes easy to use and handy for quick reference.

York Notes are ideal for:
• Essay writing
• Exam preparation
• Class discussion

The author of these Notes is David Langston MA. He is a part-time lecturer in Adult Education, a former head of English and an examiner at GCSE and Key Stage 3 for a major examination board. He has written and contributed to GCSE textbooks.

The text used in these Notes is the Arden Shakespeare, edited by T.W. Craik (Routledge, 1995).

Health Warning: This study guide will enhance your understanding, but should not replace the reading of the original text and/or study in class.

PART ONE

INTRODUCTION

HOW TO STUDY A PLAY

You have bought this book because you wanted to study a play on your own. This may supplement classwork.

- Drama is a special 'kind' of writing (the technical term is 'genre') because it needs a performance in the theatre to arrive at a full interpretation of its meaning. When reading a play you have to imagine how it should be performed; the words alone will not be sufficient. Think of gestures and movements.

- Drama is always about conflict of some sort (it may be below the surface). Identify the conflicts in the play and you will be close to identifying the large ideas or themes which bind all the parts together.

- Make careful notes on themes, characters, plot and any sub-plots of the play.

- Playwrights find non-realistic ways of allowing an audience to see into the minds and motives of their characters. The 'soliloquy', in which a character speaks directly to the audience, is one such device. Does the play you are studying have any such passages?

- Which characters do you like or dislike in the play? Why? Do your sympathies change as you see more of these characters?

- Think of the playwright writing the play. Why were these particular arrangements of events, these particular sets of characters and these particular speeches chosen?

Studying on your own requires self-discipline and a carefully thought-out work plan in order to be effective. Good luck.

Shakespeare's family

William Shakespeare was born in Stratford-upon-Avon in 1564. His father was a successful leather-worker and merchant who became an important figure in the town. It is likely that William was educated at the local grammar school where he would have been taught Latin, history, **rhetoric** (see Literary Terms) and logic (reasoning).

At the age of eighteen he married Ann Hathaway, who was twenty-six and pregnant with his child. There is little documentary evidence about Shakespeare's early life but it is thought that he moved to London around 1585.

Actor and playwright

It is recorded that in 1592 he was an actor and dramatist in London. He is listed as a performer in plays by Ben Jonson in 1598 and 1603, but it is likely that he concentrated on his own work after this.

It has not been possible to establish the exact dates when the individual plays were written but it is accepted that the history plays, including *Henry V*, appeared before 1600. Some scholars have suggested that this play was first performed in 1599, around the time of the expedition led by the Earl of Essex to suppress a rebellion in Ireland. The play completes a sequence of histories beginning with *Richard II* and continuing through *Henry IV, Part 1* and *Henry IV, Part 2*.

Shakespeare had a share in a theatre company called the Chamberlain's Men, renamed the King's Men after the accession of James I. In 1599 the company established a new theatre, the Globe, on the south bank of the Thames.

A man of property

Through the **patronage** (see Literary Terms) of the Earl of Southampton and the favour of Queen Elizabeth and later King James, the company was extremely successful. Shakespeare became a wealthy

Shakespeare man and in today's terms he could be considered a self-
achieved great made millionaire, perhaps on the scale of Paul
success. He was a McCartney or Andrew Lloyd Webber. In 1596 he
favourite at court successfully applied, on his father's behalf, for a family
and immensely coat of arms and the following year he bought New
popular with the Place, a large house in Stratford. He later invested in
public. the local brewing industry and bought land near the
town, retiring to live there around 1611. He died on 23
April, 1616, and was buried in Holy Trinity Church.

CONTEXT & SETTING

THE HISTORICAL PERSPECTIVE

The monarchy For several hundred years the position of the monarch
was seen as one ordained and approved by God. By
Shakespeare's time certainties about the God-given
order of things were being seriously challenged. The
Protestant Reformation had rejected the authority of
the Pope and his position as God's representative on
earth. The increasingly numerous wealthy merchants
were beginning to resent the privileges of the
aristocracy.

After the defeat of Queen Elizabeth I reigned from 1558 to 1603. During
the Spanish the later years of her rule, when Shakespeare was
Armada in 1588 writing his history plays, there were constant fears of
there was an plots and rebellions. Although Protestantism was the
increase in officially approved religion, there were pressures from
patriotic feeling in Protestant extremists who wished to make further
the country. reforms, such as the removal of bishops. The existence
of a large Catholic minority was also seen as a threat to
the established order. Both factions were exploited by
agents of foreign powers.

The issues of stable and legitimate monarchy, rank and
order in society, unity, loyalty, rebellion and treason are

significant themes in a number of Shakespeare's plays of this period. They were vitally relevant to the times. In *Henry V* we see the King check the legitimacy of his rights to France, act firmly on those rights, deal with treachery, unite and inspire his people and maintain a firm and just control.

Essex in Ireland

When *Henry V* was first performed, the Earl of Tyrone had recently led a rebellion against the English forces in Ireland. Queen Elizabeth appointed the popular Earl of Essex as governor of Ireland and he set off to suppress the rebels. There is a reference to his expected victorious return at the beginning of Act V, lines 29–32. Although the play is based on historical sources and is the completion of a series which begins with *Richard II*, we can see the parallel with the

Essex was cheered by the people of London as he left for Ireland.

contemporary expedition to reclaim what was considered to be the monarch's rightful domain. Henry goes to France to claim his rights and Essex goes to Ireland to do the same on behalf of the Queen.

Shakespeare's sources

The main source used by Shakespeare for the events in *Henry V* was *Chronicles of England, Scotland and Ireland* by Raphael Holinshed, first published in 1577. He also used *The Union of the Two Noble and Illustre Families of Lancaster and York* written by Edward Hall and published in 1548, and an anonymous play, *The Famous Victories of Henry the Fifth*. Although the play follows some of Holinshed's detail closely, Shakespeare gives the story life and shape through his verse and dramatic invention.

THE SOCIAL CONTEXT

Low life

In the sixteenth century, the population of London grew from 50,000 to 200,000, despite a serious outbreak of plague. It was a centre of trade and commerce and also a focus for those who wished to find favour at court. At the other end of the social scale it was home to a large criminal underclass of thieves, professional beggars, swindlers, prostitutes, pimps and brothel-keepers.

In *Henry IV, Part 1* and *Part 2*, Shakespeare shows us his familiarity with this underworld through his amusing portraits of the low-life characters. Some of these characters survive in *Henry V* and see the military campaign as an opportunity to extend their thieving into new pastures.

The Theatre   By the time *Henry V* was performed, the theatre in London was well established but operated under some difficulties. The court welcomed new drama and patronised the playwrights and players, but the Puritan local authorities disapproved. They considered plays and play-acting to be immoral and they believed that the playhouses attracted criminals and encouraged lewd behaviour. Public performances were usually held outside the city boundaries in inn yards and later in purpose-built theatres like the Globe. The profession of acting was not recognised in law and actors could be treated as vagabonds who had no visible means of support. It was therefore important that they came under the patronage and protection of powerful people.

PART TWO

SUMMARIES

GENERAL SUMMARY

Prologue   The Chorus asks the audience to excuse the limitations of the theatre and to use their imaginations to conjure up the great events which are to be presented in the play.

Act I   The Archbishop of Canterbury and the Bishop of Ely are concerned about a proposed bill which would transfer a great deal of the Church's property to the King. The Archbishop hopes that he may have averted this by the offer of a large sum of money. We hear that the King's character has greatly improved since he has come to the throne.

The two churchmen are called before the King to give their expert opinion on his claim to the crown of France. They give historical and legal reasons why his claim is valid and encourage him to go to France and seize what is his. Some of the nobles present support this view and, after considering the danger of a Scottish invasion, Henry decides to invade France.

Ambassadors from the Dauphin deliver a rejection of his claims to territory in France and an insulting gift in the form of tennis balls. Henry sends a menacing reply, saying that the Dauphin will bear responsibility for a great deal of death and destruction. He tells his nobles to prepare for war.

Act II   The Chorus describes the excitement as the army gets ready to depart from Southampton, but warns that there are traitors in the English ranks.

We witness a quarrel between some of the low-life characters in London and learn that Sir John Falstaff, an old drinking companion of the King, is ill.

At Southampton, King Henry exposes three traitors and sentences them to death. He then calls on his lords to follow him to France.

Meanwhile Falstaff has died and the low-life characters, Pistol, Bardolph and Nym, along with a boy servant, are leaving to join the army, hoping to profit from the war.

At the French court, King Charles is organising the defence of his country. His son, the Dauphin, believes that the English are not a serious threat and that Henry is a vain and weak youth. The Constable of France disagrees and warns him not to underestimate the English King. Exeter, as ambassador, delivers Henry's demand for the French crown. The alternative is war.

Act III

The Chorus describes the English invasion fleet and the siege of the French town of Harfleur and mentions that the French King has offered Henry his daughter in marriage along with some land.

King Henry rallies his men for an assault on Harfleur. Some of the low-life characters are reluctant to advance and are encouraged by Fluellen, a Welsh captain, who is then involved in a comical argument with an Irish, a Scots and an English captain.

Henry warns the Governor of Harfleur of the death and destruction that will follow if he does not surrender. The Governor agrees to open the gates and the Duke of Exeter is put in command of the town.

At the French court, Princess Katherine tries to learn some English from her maid.

The French King discusses Henry's progress with his nobles. He orders them to move against the English and defeat them.

In the English camp, Pistol falls out with Captain
Fluellen because the latter refuses to intercede for
Bardolph, who is to be hanged for theft. The French
King sends a herald to Henry with terms for his
surrender and ransom. Henry says that he does not seek
a fight but will do so if he and his army are prevented
from reaching Calais.

The night before battle, the French nobles boast to
each other about their equipment and horses.
They are so confident they begin to pity the
English.

Act IV   The Chorus describes the scene as the two armies wait
for the morning. King Henry moves round the camp
visiting his men. He borrows a cloak and in this
disguise he sounds out the feelings of some common
soldiers. He is conscious of his great responsibility and
prays for God's support.

In the morning the French nobles, full of confidence,
leave their camp for the battlefield.

The English lords wish each other good luck and
Henry addresses them, saying that the day will go down
in history and that those who stayed in England will
always regret that they were not present at the battle.
Once again he rejects an offer of personal ransom from
the French and he urges his men forward.

We are shown a number of short scenes from the
battle:

Pistol captures a French soldier.

The French nobles are shocked and ashamed by their
lack of success.

We hear of the brave deaths of two English nobles and
of the cowardly slaughter by the French of the boys
who were with the English army's baggage.

The French herald comes to concede defeat and to ask Henry's permission to gather the dead. We hear details of the French prisoners and of the dead of both sides. Henry gives orders for prayers to be said and for the army's return to England.

Act V   The Chorus tells us of Henry's enthusiastic reception in London. He then asks us to skip over the intervening events (in fact a period of four years) and, like Henry, return to France.

Fluellen takes revenge on Pistol for insulting him. Pistol, the only survivor of the low-life characters, decides to return to England to make a dishonest living. King Henry and his nobles meet with the French and they exchange polite greetings. Henry leaves his advisors to discuss the peace terms with the French King while he talks to Princess Katherine. Their conversation is partly comical because of the language barrier but he wins her consent to be his wife. The King of France agrees to the terms and to his daughter's marriage to King Henry with the hope that there will be peace between the two countries.

Epilogue   The Chorus closes with an apology for the shortcomings of the drama. We are told that King Henry's gains were lost in the reign of his son Henry VI.

DETAILED SUMMARIES

ACT I

CHORUS   The play opens with a Prologue spoken by the Chorus. He calls for inspiration to help show the great events and heroic characters involved in the story which is to be presented. He asks the audience to make allowances for the limitations of the small theatre and encourages them to use their imaginations to conjure up the large number of men and horses involved in the battles.

COMMENT   The Chorus was used in classical Greek drama to comment on the action and usually consisted of a group of actors. In this play, the Chorus is spoken by a single actor.

Shakespeare wishes to impress his audience that this is an epic story they are about to see and he enlists their help in its creation.

GLOSSARY   **Muse** the Muses were Greek goddesses of creative arts
Assume the port of Mars take on the mannerisms of Mars, the Roman god of war
cockpit the theatre is being compared to a circular pit used for the sport of cock-fighting
casques helmets
puissance forces, armies or power in general

SCENE 1   The Archbishop of Canterbury and the Bishop of Ely are discussing the re-introduction of a government bill which will strip the Church of a great deal of its wealth.

The churchmen are skilful politicians.   The Archbishop takes some comfort in the fact that the King seems to be in sympathy with them and has been offered a substantial gift of money.

We hear that Henry is a persuasive speaker.   We hear that the King's character has reformed since he has come to the throne and that he is widely admired and respected for his scholarship and his skill in debate.

The Archbishop also mentions the King's claims to the crown of France and the presence of French Ambassadors at the court.

COMMENT   We see that the churchmen have a strong motive for encouraging the King's claims in France. If they finance the war, it will turn attention away from the bill which has been proposed.

The description of the changes in King Henry's character remind the audience of his wild and reckless behaviour as Prince Hal in the previous two plays in the series, *Henry IV, Part 1* and *Part 2*. The audience will be interested to see this reformed King living up to the promises he made in *Henry IV, Part 1* (Act I, Scene 2).

The main plot of the King's claim to the crown of France is introduced and we anticipate the confrontation between Henry and the French Ambassadors.

GLOSSARY

scambling quarrelsome, unsettled

lazars lepers and other diseased people

currence current, flowing

Hydra-headed many-headed, the Hydra was a nine-headed monster in Greek mythology

Gordian knot a complex problem, the Gordian knot was extremely intricate and could not be undone but Alexander the Great cut it with his sword

chartered libertine one given freedom to go anywhere

riots loose-living, revelry

sequestration keeping apart

crescive growing

SCENE 2

The Church must share responsibility for the war.

King Henry sends for the Archbishop of Canterbury and asks him for his considered opinion on his legal rights to his claims in France. He warns the Archbishop that a great deal of blood may be shed as a consequence of his advice.

The Archbishop gives a detailed history of the kingdoms of France and Germany. He argues that the Salic law, which excludes succession through the female line and which has been used by the French to deny Henry's claim, is valid only in Germany and does not apply in France.

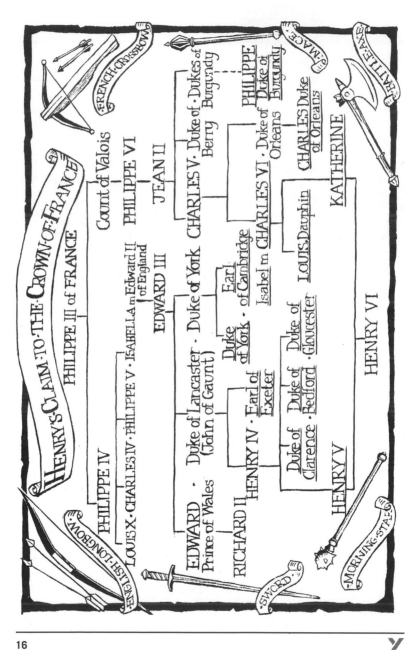

The King is reminded of the deeds of Edward III and the Black Prince.

Henry asks the Archbishop to confirm his right to make the claim, which he does, reminding him of his ancestors' victories against the French and promising a generous donation from the Church.

Some of the nobles present add their encouragement. The King then considers the possibility that the Scots may take advantage of his absence and invade. The Archbishop, using as a metaphor the diverse but cooperative functions of bees in a bee-hive, suggests that the King divides his forces into four and takes one quarter with him to France. Henry says he is determined to rule France or to die in the attempt.

The French Ambassadors are shown in. They are from the Dauphin, son of the French King. Henry assures them that they may speak plainly. The Dauphin's message is an insulting rejection of Henry's claims to French dukedoms and contains references to the English King's former reputation as a trivial pleasure-seeker. This message is accompanied by a mocking gift of tennis balls.

Henry turns the Dauphin's tennis balls' insult against him.

King Henry takes up the theme of tennis in his reply and warns that a deadly game will follow. He says that his life so far has merely been preparation for taking his place on the throne of France. The Dauphin's mockery will bring much misery and hardship on the French people as Henry intends to proceed in a just cause.

When the Ambassadors are dismissed Henry tells his followers to direct all their energies to preparing the expedition.

COMMENT

King Henry wants religious and legal support for his claim. He makes the Archbishop share the responsibility for the proposed war.

The Archbishop gives his legal opinion but also encourages Henry with references to his heroic ancestors. Both the Archbishop and the Bishop of Ely use bloodthirsty images.

Henry shows that he is a cautious and responsible ruler when he considers the danger of a Scottish invasion.

Henry's reply to the Dauphin's message shows dignity, self-control and wit. There is also a cold, menacing determination in his speech.

We are given the impression of nobles and Church being united behind an intelligent and formidable young monarch.

GLOSSARY

nicely paying too much attention to detail

impawn put at risk

conjuration serious appeal

defunction death

embare uncover

pavilioned camped in tents

marches border areas

coursing snatchers thieves on horseback

giddy unpredictable

Congreeing agreeing together

Gallia France

galliard a dance

wrangler quarrelsome person

proportions arrangements of troops, equipment and money

TEST YOURSELF (Act I)

A *Identify the speaker.*

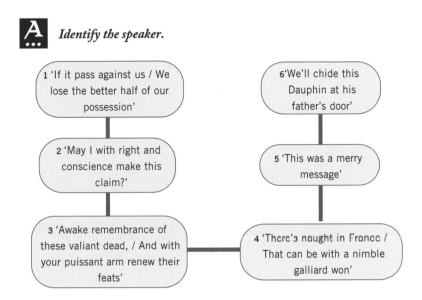

1 'If it pass against us / We lose the better half of our possession'

2 'May I with right and conscience make this claim?'

3 'Awake remembrance of these valiant dead, / And with your puissant arm renew their feats'

4 'There's nought in France / That can be with a nimble galliard won'

5 'This was a merry message'

6 'We'll chide this Dauphin at his father's door'

Identify the person 'to whom' this comment refers.

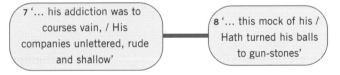

7 '... his addiction was to courses vain, / His companies unlettered, rude and shallow'

8 '... this mock of his / Hath turned his balls to gun-stones'

Check your answers on page 79.

B *Consider these issues.*

a The motives and the behaviour of the two churchmen.

b What we are told about the King's character.

c The way in which King Henry uses the Archbishop of Canterbury.

d How the King shows his qualities of leadership.

e The relationship between the King and his nobles, as seen in Act I, Scene 2.

f The effect the Dauphin's message is likely to have on the audience.

ACT II

CHORUS

King Henry is in danger in his own country.

The Chorus tells us about the excitement and anticipation in England as the King and his followers prepare for war. We learn that the French have bribed three English traitors to murder Henry before he sets sail. When we next see the King he will be in Southampton.

COMMENT

The business-like preparations of the English contrast with the vanity and show of the French nobles later in the play.

The audience will be curious about the outcome of the murder plot.

GLOSSARY

dalliance idle, time-wasting pleasures
Mercuries Mercury was messenger of the gods, represented with wings on his shoes and his hat
gilt gold, allows the **pun** (see Literary Terms) on 'guilt'

SCENE 1

In a street

Bardolph and Nym, two of the old drinking companions of King Henry's youth, meet and discuss Nym's quarrel with Pistol, another low-life character. Pistol is married to Nell Quickly, hostess of a tavern, who had previously been engaged to Nym. These three rogues call each other by military ranks as they are about to set off on the expedition to France.

When Pistol enters with his wife, he and Nym exchange extravagant and ludicrous insults and threaten to fight each other. Bardolph comes between them.

News of Falstaff's illness reminds the audience how the King has changed.

A boy servant enters with news that his master is very ill and begs them to come to him. (His master is Sir John Falstaff another of the King's old drinking companions now cast off by the reformed and responsible monarch.) The Hostess leaves with the Boy and Bardolph establishes a truce between Pistol and

Nym. The Hostess returns and begs them to come to the sick Sir John. It is suggested that he is suffering from a broken heart because of the King's treatment of him.

COMMENT These low-life characters bring humour to the play and their scenes provide light relief from the serious events of the main plot.

The audience is reminded of the King's wild youth by the presence of these old companions who serve to underline the great changes in his behaviour and bearing.

Pistol speaks in a bombastic, comical kind of verse. It is a windy parody of **epic** style, full of **alliteration** (see Literary Terms) and suits his boastful, empty bravado.

GLOSSARY   **Ancient** ensign, standard-bearer

wink close both eyes

iron sword

rendezvous a place of escape

troth-plight engaged to be married

tyke dog

shog off go away

solus singly

egregious outrageous

maw stomach

Barbason the name of a devil

wight man

mickle much

Couple a gorge false French for 'Cut the throat'

spital leper-house

kite bird of prey, here meaning a prostitute

Cressid Cressida, a fictional character who was afflicted with leprosy by the gods

espouse marry

quondam previous

noble one-third of a pound

sutler seller of provisions
quotidian tertian type of fever
fracted broken

SCENE

At Southampton

There are hidden meanings in Henry's words to the traitors.

Some of the English lords are discussing the villainy of the traitors in their midst when the King enters in the company of the three conspirators. He asks their opinion of the prospects for his invasion of France. They answer with encouraging words and he says he will not forget to reward people according to their deserts.

Henry orders the release of a drunk who was arrested for shouting insults about him in the streets, but the traitors protest that he is being too lenient. He then hands the traitors written orders which are in fact details of their treachery. They immediately fall on their knees and submit to his mercy. Henry says that they have just advised him against being too merciful. He denounces them for their treason, particularly Lord Scroop who had been close to him and in whom he had confided a great deal.

The traitors seem glad they have been discovered.

The traitors repent and accept their fate. King Henry sentences them to death and they are taken away to be executed. The discovery of the plot is seen by Henry as a sign that God is on his side and he orders the immediate departure of the invasion fleet.

COMMENT At the beginning of the scene we share the knowledge with the King and his lords that the plot has been discovered and we are anxious to see how the traitors will be exposed and how they will react.

Henry shows his command of the situation by playing with the traitors.

We see that Henry is firm in his punishment of serious crimes and confident enough be merciful in the case of the drunk.

GLOSSARY

powers forces
galls bitterness
quittance repayment
railed shouted abuse
orisons prayers
distemper illness
winked at ignored
practices plots
yoke-devils devils working as if they were harnessed together like horses or oxen
admiration amazement
wrought worked
dub award a title
gulled tricked
Tartar Tartarus, the darkest part of Hell
affiance trust
boulted sifted
golden earnest advance payment in gold
rub problem, obstacle

SCENE 3

Falstaff died repenting his sins.

Pistol, Bardolph, Nym and the Boy are leaving London to join the army. Pistol's wife, the Hostess, is seeing them off and she gives a pathetic and comic account of the death of Falstaff. Pistol warns her to take good care of business. The rogues leave for France with the intention of profiting from the war.

COMMENT Falstaff's death marks the end of an era. He was the leader and the inspiration of this band of thieves and rogues.

This scene provides another short relief from the serious action.

Pistol's image of going to France to suck blood is a suitable one as they intend to be parasites and steal what they can.

GLOSSARY **wheresome'er** wheresoever
'A dialect for 'he'
christom child a newly-christened baby
stone can also mean testicle
sack a dry Spanish wine
Whore of Babylon the scarlet woman of the Book of Revelation (17:4–5)
shog depart
wafer-cakes thin biscuits, easily broken
Caveto beware
crystals eyes
horse-leeches large blood-sucking worms

SCENE 4

The French court
The Dauphin is over-confident and arrogant.

The French King orders his nobles and his son to strengthen the defences against the English invasion. The Dauphin agrees that precautions should be taken but refuses to accept that the English King is a serious threat. He brushes aside a warning from the Constable of France who believes that Henry has changed. His father the King treats the invasion as a grave danger and refers to previous English successes.

The Duke of Exeter arrives as Ambassador for King Henry. He demands that Charles surrenders the crown of France and he hands him a family tree which proves the justice of Henry's claim. Refusal will bring about

Is King Charles's delay weakness or caution? great suffering and death. King Charles says he will give his answer on the following day.

Exeter then tells the Dauphin that King Henry wishes him to know that he will regret his insulting gift.

Comment   King Charles is cautious and weak. He does not inspire his followers, instead he talks of fears and old defeats.

The Dauphin's defiance is based on ignorance and prejudice.

We see here the first signs of disunity among the French.

Exeter is bold and confident. Unlike the French Ambassadors, he does not hesitate to deliver his message.

We are again reminded that Henry has cast off his previous idle ways. This builds up our anticipation to see him in action.

GLOSSARY   **defendant** defensive

meet appropriate, correct

humorous changeable, fickle

forespent exhausted, finished with

Brutus Lucius Junius Brutus pretended to be mad to cover his plot against the King of Rome

Cressy Crécy, a battle in 1346, won by Edward III and his son, the Black Prince, so named because of his black armour

sinister clumsy, twisted, left-handed

Jove ruler of the gods, thunderbolts were his weapons

second accent echo

ordinance artillery

Paris-balls tennis balls

Paris Louvre a royal palace at the time

mistress principal, most important

greener younger

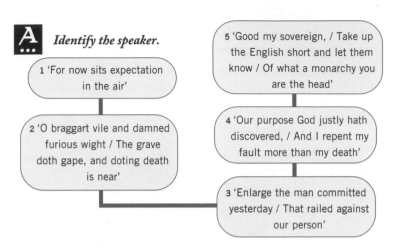

A *Identify the speaker.*

1 'For now sits expectation in the air'

2 'O braggart vile and damned furious wight / The grave doth gape, and doting death is near'

5 'Good my sovereign, / Take up the English short and let them know / Of what a monarchy you are the head'

4 'Our purpose God justly hath discovered, / And I repent my fault more than my death'

3 'Enlarge the man committed yesterday / That railed against our person'

Identify the person 'to whom' this comment refers.

6 'That he should for a foreign purse so sell / His sovereign's life to death and treachery!'

7 'Nay, sure, he's not in hell; he's in Arthur's bosom, if ever a man went to Arthur's bosom'

8 'a vain, giddy, shallow, humorous youth'

Check your answers on page 79.

B *Consider these issues.*

a The effectiveness of the Chorus's description of the invasion preparations.

b Scenes 1 and 3 provide humorous diversions from the main plot but also give us glimpses of the King's discarded companions and thus a reminder of his old way of life. There is also an element of sadness involved.

c Consider the way in which King Henry controls the situation in Scene 2.

d Look at the French King's responses to the invasion and to Henry's demands and consider the differences in the characters of the two monarchs.

e The differences between the language of the court and that used by the low-life characters. Pistol's speech is different from that of the other rogues.

f Relationships between members of the French court, as seen in Act II, Scene 4.

ACT III

CHORUS

Henry is not to be bought off at this stage.

The Chorus asks the audience to imagine they have watched the English fleet, like a floating city, sailing towards Harfleur. We are told of the siege of that town and the French King's offer of his daughter in marriage together with some dukedoms. Henry has rejected the offer and the siege continues.

COMMENT

The Chorus is used to help create the sense of spectacle and the movement of great forces. He also gives us historical information which helps us to understand later events.

This is the first we hear of Princess Katherine and the suggestion of a marriage between her and Henry.

GLOSSARY

Phoebus another name for Apollo the sun god
hempen rope
threaden made of thread
rivage shore
sternage astern, to the rear
pith and puissance strength and power
culled picked
linstock staff to hold the lighted match the gunner will set to a cannon

SCENE 1

We see that Henry leads from the front.

At the siege of Harfleur, King Henry rallies his men for one more attack on the town. He calls on them to summon up their most fierce and aggressive qualities and reminds them of the victories of their forefathers.

COMMENT

To achieve his purpose Henry uses several approaches in his speech:
- He calls his men 'dear friends', implying that they are his willing companions

- He prompts his nobles to live up to the exploits of their forefathers and to set an example to people of more common blood
- He flatters the ordinary soldiers (yeomen) with the suggestion that he sees 'noble' qualities shining in their eyes
- He makes the battle seem exciting by comparing it to a hunt

GLOSSARY

portage opening
galled uneven, worn away
jutty stick out
fet fetched, derived from
be copy be an example
grosser more common
the game's afoot the hunted animal is running

SCENE *2*

Bardolph, Nym and Pistol are worthless as soldiers.

Bardolph leads the low-life characters at the tail-end of the attack, but Nym, Pistol and the Boy are reluctant to go any further. Fluellen, a Welsh captain, arrives and drives the three rogues forward. The Boy is left on stage. He says that he is tired of working for such cowards and thieves and he plans to find better employment.

We hear about the technical work involved in the siege.

Fluellen returns and meets Gower, an English captain. They discuss the progress of the mines which are being dug to blow up the town walls. Fluellen expresses contempt for captain Macmorris, an Irishman, who is in charge of the work. Macmorris arrives with captain Jamy, a Scotsman, and a comical discussion follows. Captain Gower is trying to keep the peace between Fluellen and Macmorris when they are interrupted by the sound of a trumpet-call from the town.

COMMENT

We witness the cowardly behaviour of the rogues and their undignified retreat from Fluellen's anger.

We have some sympathy for the Boy as he says he does not wish to be corrupted by the thieves.

Shakespeare's audience would have found the language of the captains amusing. They are national stereotypes. The fact that they are having a serious dispute about the technical aspects of warfare in their comic dialects adds to the humour.

The presence of English, Irish, Scots and Welsh captains suggests a broad base of British support for Henry which is not historically sound, but reflects the political circumstances of Shakespeare's time. The captains take their work seriously and are loyal soldiers.

GLOSSARY

God's vassals God's servants, men

cullions rascals

bawcock fine fellow

swashers boastful cowards

antics clowns

th'athversary adversary, opponent

Chesu Jesus

plow up blow up

falarous valorous

God-den Good even, evening (used as a greeting after mid-day)

pioneers sappers, miners

mess mass
lig i'th' grund lie in the ground
breff brief, short

SCENE 3

At the gate of
Harfleur
Henry paints a
fearsome picture of
the sack of
Harfleur.

King Henry addresses the Governor of Harfleur. He tells him that this is his last chance to surrender and describes in vivid terms the destruction and murder which will follow if the English troops are let loose in the town. The Governor has been told that the Dauphin is unable to send him reinforcements and he surrenders to Henry.

The King leaves Exeter in charge of the town with instructions to be merciful to the people. His army has been weakened through sickness and he intends to withdraw to Calais for the winter.

COMMENT

Henry is seen to be both merciful towards the French people and careful with his own troops. He avoids unnecessary bloodshed.

In his speech we are given a graphic description of the brutalities of warfare.

We learn that despite this victory the English army is weak and vulnerable. The French have not yet committed their main forces.

GLOSSARY

parle parley, talk
battery bombardment
impious wicked, evil
smirched dirtied
fell feats deadly deeds
bootless uselessly
leviathan mythical sea-monster
spitted impaled, skewered
Herod King Herod ordered the murder of all children under two-years old in an attempt to get rid of Jesus (Bible, Matt. 2:16–18)

SCENE 4

At the French court

Why does Princess Katherine want to learn English?

Speaking in French, the Princess Katherine asks her maid to teach her English. The maid, whose command of English is very poor, tells her the names of parts of the body and Katherine tries to memorise them. Some of the English words sound rather indecent to French ears and the Princess is shocked.

COMMENT

The audience would be amused to hear the French characters mispronouncing English words. Even in Shakespeare's day it was easy to raise a laugh at the expense of 'funny' foreigners and their inability to speak correct English.

Those in the audience who understood French would be more amused by the Princess's response to the English words, 'gown' and 'foot', which sounded like coarse and indelicate expressions in her own language.

We have heard about Katherine as a possible bride for Henry. We now see that she is a lively good-humoured young woman.

SCENE 5

The French nobles are concerned with their personal honour.

The French continue to underestimate the English.

The Dauphin and the French nobles are eager to attack the English. They are angry and insulted by the presence of Henry's troops and express contempt for the cold and damp little island they have come from. According to the Dauphin the French ladies have begun to mock their menfolk for their lack of courage.

The French King orders his nobles to attack the English and to capture Henry but refuses to allow the Dauphin to go with the army. The Constable of France regrets that, because the English army is so small and weak, Henry will probably surrender without a fight.

COMMENT

The French despise the English and consider their royalty to be an illegitimate offshoot of France, 'Norman bastards'.

They describe the country and the climate in insulting terms. The audience will be eager to see them humbled.

The French use casual oaths in their conversation unlike Henry who is pious and dignified in his speech.

King Charles's list of the French nobility who are to attack the English is echoed later in the list of the dead and prisoners after Agincourt (Act IV, Scene 8).

GLOSSARY
O Dieu vivant! O living God!
sprays shoots, small branches
luxury vice, lust
Mort de ma vie Death of my life, a common French oath
slobbery slimy, muddy
nook-shotten full of crooked corners
Albion the island of Britain
Dieu de batailles God of battles
mettle strength of character
drench medicine
sur-reined jades overworked horses
Decoct boil
lavoltas, corantos dances which included turning and running movements
void his rheum spit out his phlegm

SCENE 6

The English camp

Bardolph has come to the end of his career of crime.

Fluellen meets captain Gower and tells him about some fighting he has been involved in, defending a bridge with the Duke of Exeter. He says that he noted the bravery of one particular man in the action. This turns out to be Pistol who arrives to ask Fluellen to go to the Duke of Exeter and intercede for Bardolph who is about to be hanged for stealing from a church. Fluellen believes in strict discipline and refuses to interfere. Pistol curses him and leaves. Gower says he recognises Pistol for a well-known rogue, and the kind of man who will return to England and live off his tales of the war. Fluellen agrees that Pistol had deceived him.

King Henry enters and Fluellen reports the Duke of Exeter's successful action at the bridge. When asked about English casualties Fluellen says that the only loss is a man called Bardolph, about to be hanged for theft.

Henry knows it makes sense to treat the French people gently.

Even though this was one of his old companions Henry expresses his approval and orders that there is to be no theft from or abuse of the French people.

Montjoy, the French herald, arrives with a message from the King of France. King Charles wishes to know how much Henry is prepared to pay in ransom, though he doubts if the English can afford to raise a sum which would compensate for the damage they have done. He also maintains that Henry has betrayed his followers by leading them to their doom in France.

Henry compliments Montjoy on his conduct and bearing and sends a very honest reply to King Charles.

Henry no longer appears to be the aggressor as he is trying to avoid a fight.

He says that his army is weakened through sickness and he wishes to avoid a fight and return to Calais. However he will fight if anyone stands in his way. After Montjoy leaves, Henry expresses the view that they are in God's hands and orders his men to make camp.

COMMENT

Fluellen's report of the action at the bridge helps to give the impression of a moving campaign and the feeling that the audience is seeing part of a larger series of events.

The decline of Henry's old companions is almost complete with Bardolph's execution for this most despicable petty theft. The King's ready support for the hanging shows how completely he has turned his back on the low life.

Montjoy is one of the French characters who gains our respect. Henry admires his courage and dignity.

Henry shows some of his kingly qualities in this scene. He is firm in imposing discipline in his army, generous in his praise of good conduct, even in an enemy, honest in his dealings with King Charles, humble and pious in his trust in God and brave and defiant in the face of danger.

GLOSSARY

Agamemnon King of Mycenae in the Trojan Wars
muffler scarf, blindfold
pax a tablet of precious metal with a holy picture or emblem, kissed by the priest and congregation during church services
fico fig, an insult, usually accompanied by a snap of the fingers
fig of Spain an insult as above
bawd procurer of prostitutes
sconce defensive position
find a hole in his coat get a chance to expose him
impeachment hindrance

SCENE 7

At night in the French camp

Rambures is tempting fate.

Some of the nobles are boasting about their horses and armour. They are waiting impatiently for morning and expect an easy victory over the English. The Dauphin, who has now joined the campaign, tries to outdo the others in praise of his horse and the conversation turns into an idle exchange of witticisms. One of the nobles, Rambures, suggests a game of dice for the ransoms of the prisoners they expect to capture. After the Dauphin leaves to put on his armour, the Constable expresses doubts about his bravery.

The English are compared to foolish fighting dogs.

A messenger reports that the English are camped nearby. The Constable expresses pity for King Henry and both he and Orleans feel that it is sheer stupidity that keeps the English from running away. Orleans anticipates a rich haul of prisoners.

COMMENT

There is no obvious leader among the French forces. The Dauphin, who is the most senior in rank, does not have the wholehearted support or respect of his nobles.

The Constable's remarks about the Dauphin are quite witty but they are destructive and show he has no confidence in the royal prince.

The French are passing their time in idle boasting and gossip. This contrasts with the serious and practical approach of King Henry.

The overconfidence of the French extends to anticipating the number of English prisoners.

The French use images of animals when discussing the English soldiers which suggests they think of them as being less than human.

GLOSSARY   Ch'ha! an exclamation

le cheval volant the flying horse

Pegasus a winged horse in Greek mythology

qui a les narines de feu who has nostrils of fire

Hermes in Greek mythology Hermes was able to charm people to sleep by playing his pipe

Perseus hero of Greek mythology

palfrey a riding horse, not a war-horse

kern Irish foot-soldier

strossers trousers

jade a derogatory term for a woman or a horse

A *Identify the speaker.*

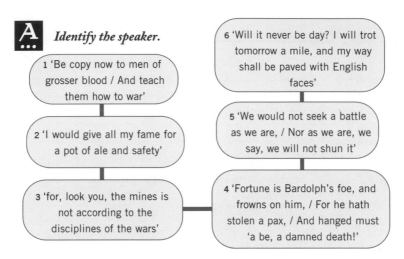

1 'Be copy now to men of grosser blood / And teach them how to war'

2 'I would give all my fame for a pot of ale and safety'

3 'for, look you, the mines is not according to the disciplines of the wars'

6 'Will it never be day? I will trot tomorrow a mile, and my way shall be paved with English faces'

5 'We would not seek a battle as we are, / Nor as we are, we say, we will not shun it'

4 'Fortune is Bardolph's foe, and frowns on him, / For he hath stolen a pax, / And hanged must 'a be, a damned death!'

Identify the person 'to whom' this comment refers.

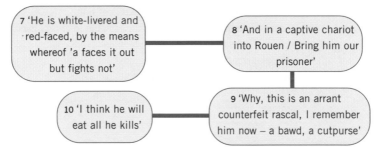

7 'He is white-livered and red-faced, by the means whereof 'a faces it out but fights not'

8 'And in a captive chariot into Rouen / Bring him our prisoner'

10 'I think he will eat all he kills'

9 'Why, this is an arrant counterfeit rascal, I remember him now – a bawd, a cutpurse'

Check your answers on page 79.

B *Consider these issues.*

a King Henry's skills in encouraging his troops at Harfleur.

b The humour in the conversation between the captains.

c The qualities shown by King Henry in his orders to his army and his reply to the French King.

d Your impressions of the French nobility.

e The dramatic purpose of Act III, Scene 2.

f The English are the invaders, but we are encouraged to see them as the underdogs.

ACT IV

CHORUS

*The name 'Harry'
emphasises the
King's friendly
relationship with
his men.*

The Chorus describes the sights and sounds of the night before the battle as the two armies are camped near each other. He contrasts the overconfident French with the war-weary English who seem like ghosts. We hear that Henry is visiting his soldiers and that his confident and friendly manner gives them comfort. The Chorus again asks our pardon for presenting such great events with such limited resources.

COMMENT

The Chorus's description compensates for the limitations of the Shakespearean theatre. The plays were performed in daylight with few sound effects and little or no scenery.

The unequal nature of the coming contest is emphasised, as is the difference in attitude between the boastful French and the weary but patient English.

Henry's relationship with his troops is seen as friendly, comforting and inspiring. His glance is like a ray of sunshine.

GLOSSARY

entertain conjecture imagine
poring eye-straining
paly pale
umbered darkened
tardy-gaited slow-paced
enrounded surrounded
attaint weariness
largess gift
foils light fencing swords

SCENE 1

At night

King Henry is discussing with the Duke of Gloucester the dangerous position they are in when they meet the Duke of Bedford and Sir Thomas Erpingham, an

There is no boasting among the English leaders.

elderly knight. Henry talks cheerfully to them and borrows Sir Thomas's cloak. He sends them to tell the other lords to meet him in his tent.

When the others have left Henry is challenged by Pistol. He does not reveal his identity and claims to be a Welshman. This causes Pistol to brag about what he intends to do to Fluellen and when Henry claims to be Fluellen's kinsman, he insults him and leaves.

Fluellen and Gower then enter. Gower greets Fluellen who tells him at great length to talk less because of the nearness of the enemy. They leave without seeing Henry.

Henry approves of Fluellen.

Three ordinary soldiers, Court, Bates and Williams, enter. Dawn is breaking and they view it with apprehension. When they see Henry he pretends to be a soldier under Sir Thomas Erpingham's command. They discuss the King and his responsibilities. Bates thinks the King would rather be up to the neck in the River Thames than here in France. Henry disagrees. Bates then says he would prefer that the King was on his own and could be ransomed without loss of life. Henry says that he would be happy to die with the King because his cause is just.

The common soldiers will be killed. They have no value as prisoners.

Bates and Williams say that they are there because they are the King's subjects and that this absolves them from any responsibility for whether the cause is just or not. The King will carry the responsibility if any of his men die in sin. Henry argues that each man is responsible to God for his own sins and the state of his soul and should therefore prepare himself before the battle so that he may die in a state of grace or live on as an example to others.

Williams expresses doubts about the King's intention to refuse personal ransom to save his life and he and Henry quarrel over this. They agree to settle their differences after the battle and exchange gloves which they will wear in their hats so as to recognise one another. Bates reminds them that they have enough French enemies to deal with.

When the soldiers leave Henry speaks his thoughts about the heavy burdens of kingship. He questions the value of ceremony and the trappings of royalty and compares the uneasy responsibilities of power with the simple, irresponsible life of the slave who can sleep peacefully each night.

We are reminded of events which took place in Richard II.

Sir Thomas Erpingham arrives to tell Henry that his nobles are looking for him. He says he will meet them at his tent. Alone again Henry prays to God to give his soldiers courage. He asks God not to punish him on this particular day for the sins of his father. (Henry IV had deposed Richard II who was later murdered.) Henry says he has done his best to compensate for this. He has wept, paid for prayers to be said and has built two chapels dedicated to Richard. He promises to do more. The Duke of Gloucester comes to take him to the meeting.

COMMENT

We see the friendly relationship between Henry and his nobles and his obvious affection for the elderly Sir Thomas.

Pistol and Fluellen provide a little humour to lighten this rather brooding and reflective scene. We can anticipate sparks when these two meet again.

There is simple comedy in Fluellen's long-winded explanation as to why Gower should keep quiet. Gower is the straight man in these scenes involving the captains.

We are given some insight into the views of the common soldiers and we are reminded that their deaths would leave their families destitute.

Our respect for Henry is enhanced because we know he takes his responsibilities seriously and is not merely pursuing personal gain and honour.

He speaks to his soldiers man to man and does not take refuge in his rank and power, even when he is threatened with violence.

Henry is pious. He prays sincerely and has tried to make amends for his father's sins.

This scene provides a slow and sombre prelude to the excitement and activity of the battle.

GLOSSARY

likes me pleases me
legerity quickness
Che vous là? Qui va là? Who goes there?
bully fine fellow
Pompey the Great Roman leader and general who lived 106–48BC
coxcomb fool
rawly at a tender age
unspotted without sin
beadle parish constable
elder-gun pop-gun made from an elder branch
gage pledge, proof of the agreement
farced stuffed, padded out
Elysium heaven, contentment
Hyperion mythical name for the sun
wots knows
jealous anxious
compassing obtaining

SCENE 2

The French camp, the next morning

It is morning and the French lords are preparing confidently for battle. A messenger informs them that the English army is in position. The Constable remarks that there are scarcely enough English to give them a decent battle. He fears that the enemy will be so overwhelmed by their approach that they will surrender

It is ironic that the French are worried they will not have a decent fight.

without a fight. The Earl of Grandpré enters and calls upon the French nobles to hurry. He describes the English as miserable and disgusting in their appearance. The Dauphin mockingly suggests that they feed and clothe the enemy before they fight them. Led by the Constable they head for the battlefield.

COMMENT   Henry is a competent general and has drawn up his forces before the French are ready. He has chosen the ground.

We are again reminded of the great French advantage in numbers and the weakness of the English forces.

Once again, the arrogance and contempt of the French lords help to increase the audience's anticipation of their defeat and humiliation.

GLOSSARY   *Monte à cheval!* To horse!

varlet laquais rascal servant

Via, les eaux et terre! Away, waters and earth!

Rien puis? L'air et feu? Nothing afterwards? Air and fire?

Cieux heavens

dout blind

curtle-axe short sword, cutlass

hilding worthless

curtains contemptuous term for their banners

beaver visor of a helmet

gimmaled jointed

guidon a pointed flag, pennant

SCENE 3

The English army, the same morning

The English leaders are assembled before the battle. We hear that King Henry has gone to view the enemy forces. His army is outnumbered by five to one. The Earl of Salisbury leaves to take up his position and bids a friendly farewell to the others.

When the King returns Westmorland says he wishes they had another ten thousand men. Henry disagrees

Henry appeals to his nobles' desire for honour and glory.

and points out that the smaller their army the greater the honour will be if they win. To emphasise this point he offers free passage home for any man who wishes to leave. He tells them that this is the feast day of St Crispian and promises that those who survive will never forget it. On the anniversary they will be proud to show their wounds and tell the story of the battle. It will be passed down in history and they will be envied by those who were not present.

Salisbury arrives to announce that the French are ready to attack. He is followed by Montjoy the herald with another enquiry about Henry's ransom price should he be captured. Henry offers nothing but his bones, if the French can manage to kill him. He sends a defiant reply to the Constable of France saying that his soldiers may look poor and dirty but their hearts are ready and willing. He tells Montjoy not to come asking about ransom again.

Before they all leave for the battlefield, Henry grants the Duke of York's request to command the vanguard.

COMMENT

Relationships between Henry and his nobles are friendly and caring.

Henry cleverly makes a virtue out their small numbers to inspire confidence in his followers.

He encourages them to think of themselves as privileged to be present. They are about to make history. He also flatters them by calling them his brothers.

He generously allows the Duke of York the honour of leading the main body of his troops.

GLOSSARY

battle army
coz cousin
Crispian patron saint of shoemakers

gentle his condition raise him to the rank of gentleman
englutted swallowed up
crazing shattering
gayness bright colours
vaward vanguard, main body of troops

SCENE 4

A quiet part
of the
battlefield

Pistol thinks that
'moi' is a coin.

During the battle Pistol captures a French soldier. They are unable to understand each other. Pistol misinterprets the Frenchman's words, and threatens him while demanding a ransom. The Boy acts as interpreter and the prisoner promises to pay two hundred crowns. Pistol leaves with his captive and the Boy comments on Pistol's loud-mouthed cowardice. We hear that Nym has been hanged as well as Bardolph. The Boy returns to the army's baggage train which, he says, is vulnerable to French attack.

COMMENT

This is a humorous interlude in the battle, made comic by the misunderstandings between Pistol and the French prisoner.

Pistol's exaggerated language and his assumed courage and ferocity are ludicrous.

The Boy's fears about the French attack on the baggage are well founded. They remind us the serious nature of the battle. He does not know he will be killed in the process.

GLOSSARY

'Caleno custore me' Pistol's garbled version of an Irish song
Perpend weigh up, consider
fox sword
egregious great
rim lining of the belly
luxurious lecherous
firk beat
Owy, cuppele gorge, permafoy Pistol's bad French for 'Yes, cut the throat, by my faith'

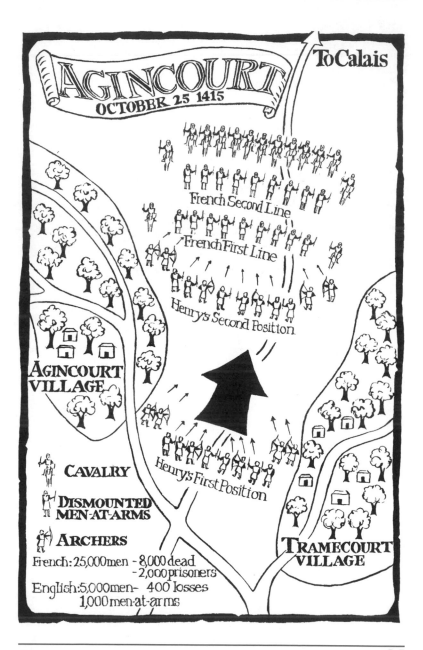

SCENE 5

During the battle

The Dauphin and the other French leaders witness with horror and shame the defeat of their forces. In despair they throw themselves into the fight hoping to salvage their honour by dying in battle.

COMMENT

The French leaders bitterly remember their boasts and how confident they were of victory. The Dauphin's suggestion that they should stab themselves is almost laughable.

They do not enter the battle to try to organise their forces but merely for reasons of damaged pride. This is a pointless act.

GLOSSARY

Fortuno thc goddoss of chance or luck
perdurable everlasting
pandar pimp, procurer of women

SCENE 6

The Duke of York is seen as an example of self-sacrifice and loyalty.

King Henry enters with his soldiers and some prisoners. He says the battle is going well but there are still French troops opposing them. Exeter arrives with a moving description of how the Duke of York was killed along with his close friend the Earl of Suffolk. A trumpet signals that the French have regrouped and the King gives orders for his men to kill their prisoners.

COMMENT

The account of the deaths of the two nobles emphasises the friendship and brotherhood among the English.

There is dramatic tension when the trumpet sounds, just when we thought the battle was won.

Henry has very practical reasons for ordering the death of the prisoners. He has a small army and he does not want his soldiers to be hindered by their captives or distracted by thoughts of ransom.

GLOSSARY

Larding feeding, enriching
Yoke-fellow they were as close as a pair of horses in harness

haggled hacked
raught reached
gripe grip
waters tears
mother tenderness, womanly feelings

SCENE 7

Another part of the battlefield

Fluellen and Gower are outraged that some of the French have attacked the English baggage train and killed the boys. They praise Henry's action in having the French prisoners killed. Fluellen is proud of Henry's Welsh connections and compares him with Alexander the Great.

Fluellen's pronunciation is confusing and comical.

Henry enters having beaten off the latest attack. The English have taken more prisoners including the Duke of Bourbon. He sees more French and sends a message to say that if they neither come and fight nor retreat then he will kill these prisoners and attack without mercy.

Montjoy arrives to ask permission for the French to retrieve their dead. He says the victory belongs to Henry who immediately praises God.

Fluellen reminds Henry of the good service of the Welsh soldiers in a previous war and Henry acknowledges Fluellen as a fellow countryman.

Henry knows Fluellen has a fiery temper.

The King sees Williams, the soldier he had quarrelled with the previous night. Williams does not recognise Henry and says he is looking for the man who wears his glove as a token so that he can box his ears. Henry, for a joke, sets up Fluellen with the glove but sends Warwick and Gloucester after him to see that no harm comes of it.

COMMENT

The French are shown in a bad light with their cowardly attack on the baggage train. It perhaps balances out against the killing of the French prisoners. Gower seems to think it is justified.

Henry can be ruthless in battle. He will do anything to keep his troops in good fighting order.

Henry once again shows his modesty and piety when he credits God with the victory and prohibits boasting on pain of death.

We also see Henry's human side as he plays the trick on Williams and Fluellen.

GLOSSARY
prains brains
porn born
void clear, vacate
skirr flee
Yerk kick
Saint Tavy's day Saint David's day
craven coward
Lucifer and Belzebub devils
jack-sauce insolent fellow
choler hot temper

SCENE 8

Fluellen, acting on Henry's information, denounces Williams as a traitor, but Henry intervenes before things take a serious turn. He gives Williams a glove full of gold in compensation.

The list of French losses illustrates the scale of the English victory.

Henry reads out a list of the French noblemen who have been taken prisoner and those who are dead. He then reads out the English losses which are very small. Again Henry thanks God, to whom he gives all credit. He gives orders for prayers to be sung before the army returns to England.

COMMENT

We may feel that it is unfair of Henry to play a trick on a humble soldier, as he has such power over him, but Williams speaks up for himself. He represents the honest, plain-spoken English yeoman.

The list of French captives and dead reminds us of Act III, Scene 5, when the French King named those who were to attack the English.

Fluellen asks Henry's permission to speak about the numbers of those killed in the battle. This is important to Fluellen as a professional soldier and a student of military history. He does not wish to boast but he likes to be in a position to put people to rights about such facts.

Henry will not take the credit for the victory. He thanks God and forbids boasting.

GLOSSARY

'Sblood God's blood, an oath

forsworn having gone back on a promise

plows blows

apprehend arrest

pear bear

prawls brawls

prabbles petty quarrels

pashful bashful, shy

of good sort of noble or high rank

Non nobis Not unto us (opening words of Psalm 115)

Te Deum O God (beginning of canticle or sung prayer)

A Identify the speaker.

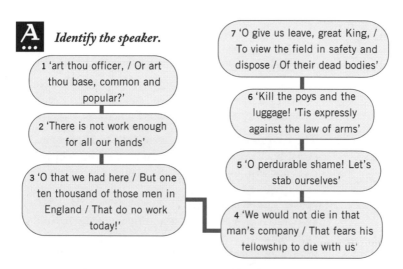

1 'art thou officer, / Or art thou base, common and popular?'

2 'There is not work enough for all our hands'

3 'O that we had here / But one ten thousand of those men in England / That do no work today!'

7 'O give us leave, great King, / To view the field in safety and dispose / Of their dead bodies'

6 'Kill the poys and the luggage! 'Tis expressly against the law of arms'

5 'O perdurable shame! Let's stab ourselves'

4 'We would not die in that man's company / That fears his fellowship to die with us'

Identify the person 'to whom' this comment refers.

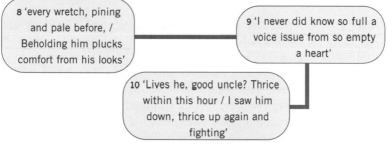

8 'every wretch, pining and pale before, / Beholding him plucks comfort from his looks'

9 'I never did know so full a voice issue from so empty a heart'

10 'Lives he, good uncle? Thrice within this hour / I saw him down, thrice up again and fighting'

Check your answers on page 79.

B Consider these issues.

a What the night before the battle shows us of Henry's character.

b The way the English nobles speak to and about each other.

c How Shakespeare creates the impression of a large-scale battle.

d The effectiveness of Henry's speech in Act IV, Scene 3, lines 19–67.

e The way the French nobles react to the prospect of defeat in Act IV, Scene 5.

f The effect of Exeter's description of the death of the Duke of York.

ACT V

CHORUS   We are told that Henry returns to England by way of
Calais and receives an enthusiastic welcome. The Holy
Roman Emperor visits England to negotiate a peace
and eventually Henry returns to France.

COMMENT   The Chorus glosses over a historical period of some
years. Shakespeare omits a number of events which he
does not wish to include in the play.

GLOSSARY   **whiffler** steward in a procession
Blackheath a common to the south-east of London. Today it is
part of London
General the Earl of Essex, sent by Queen Elizabeth to suppress
a rebellion in Ireland
Emperor the Holy Roman Emperor Sigismund
brook abridgement tolerate the brief version of events

SCENE 1   Gower asks Fluellen why he is wearing his leek when St
David's day is past. Fluellen replies that he does so to
provoke Pistol who has insulted him. Pistol arrives and
Fluellen beats him and forces him to eat the leek while
Gower denounces him as a coward. When the captains
Pistol was the last   leave, Pistol declares he will return to England to live
link with Henry's   by pimping and stealing. He will tell people that the
wild youth.   scars he received from Fluellen are war-wounds.

COMMENT   Fluellen's language and Pistol's overblown **parody**
(see Literary Terms) of heroic verse provide much of
the humour in their encounters.

The serious and responsible Gower approves of this
punishment of the cowardly and insolent rogue and
supports the Welshman.

Pistol is the last survivor of Henry's old drinking
cronies. He disappears into the criminal underworld of
London.

GLOSSARY

scald scabby, scurvy

bedlam mad

Parca the Parcae were the three Fates, the sisters in mythology, who spun, measured and cut the thread of human life

qualmish offended, nauseated

Cadwallader a Welsh king

coxcomb head

groat coin worth four pence

gleeking and galling mocking

malady of France syphilis

SCENE

The French court

The language is formal and dignified at this meeting.

King Henry, accompanied by his nobles, is welcomed by the French King and his Queen. The Duke of Burgundy, acting as intermediary, describes how warfare has laid waste much of France. Henry says that the French must agree to his demands if they want peace. The French King says he will look at these terms once more and give his answer. Henry delegates Exeter and other nobles to discuss the treaty. He is left with Princess Katherine and her maid.

Henry speaks in prose here, emphasising that he is a plain-spoken man.

Henry asks Katherine if she will have him as a husband. He claims to be nothing more than a simple soldier, a man of action and that he is unable to court her with fine words. Katherine speaks partly in French and partly in broken English. She agrees to marry him if her father wishes it. Henry assures her that he does and persuades her to allow him to kiss her.

When the others return there is some teasing from the Duke of Burgundy. The French have agreed to the English demands, including Henry's marriage to Katherine, and Henry is declared heir to the French throne. The French King and Queen express the hope that the marriage will bring unity and peace to the two countries.

COMMENT   Burgundy's speech reminds us of the real destruction and suffering caused by the war.

King Charles of France is again seen to be slow to make up his mind. This contrasts with Henry's decisive and determined nature.

It is hard to believe Henry's claim to be poor with words when we have witnessed his skill when encouraging his army, but perhaps we should admire him for his modesty.

All Henry's demands have been granted. The play ends with his complete success.

GLOSSARY   **balls** can mean eyeballs or cannon-balls or both here
basilisks dragons, also large cannons
congreeted greeted each other
even-pleached evenly plaited
mince pretend, pose affectedly
greenly sickly, as in love-sick
Saint Denis patron saint of France
scambling struggling, fighting
flower-de-luce fleur de lys, lily, emblem of the French monarchy
Plantagenet family name of the English monarchs from 1154 to 1485
naked and blind Cupid, god of love, was represented as a naked and blind boy
paction agreement, pact

EPILOGUE   The Chorus apologises for the humble efforts of the author and once again for the limitations of the small theatre in the presentation of such glorious events. He reminds the audience that Henry's gains were lost during the reign of his son, Henry VI.

COMMENT   The Chorus reminds the audience that this glorious period of English history did not last and was followed by defeat abroad and civil war at home. Shakespeare is perhaps making a point about the importance of unity and stability.

Shakespeare's plays dealing with the reign of Henry VI were first performed about ten years before he wrote *Henry V* and they would be familiar to many playgoers

GLOSSARY   **mangling** spoiling
starts short extracts
the world's best garden France
infant bands strips of linen in which babies were wrapped

A Identify the speaker.

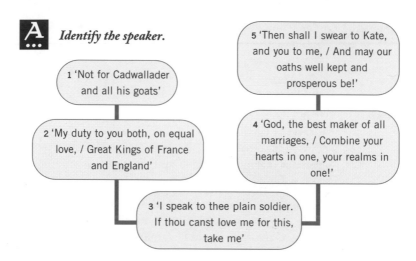

1 'Not for Cadwallader and all his goats'

2 'My duty to you both, on equal love, / Great Kings of France and England'

3 'I speak to thee plain soldier. If thou canst love me for this, take me'

4 'God, the best maker of all marriages, / Combine your hearts in one, your realms in one!'

5 'Then shall I swear to Kate, and you to me, / And may our oaths well kept and prosperous be!'

Identify the character 'to whom' this comment refers.

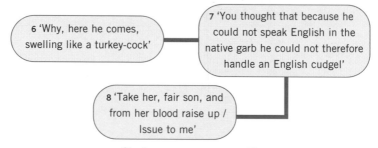

6 'Why, here he comes, swelling like a turkey-cock'

7 'You thought that because he could not speak English in the native garb he could not therefore handle an English cudgel'

8 'Take her, fair son, and from her blood raise up / Issue to me'

Check your answers on page 79.

B Consider these issues.

a The kinds of humour in Scene 1; character, language and situation.

b The different aspects of Henry's character as he deals with the treaty and with Katherine.

c The effectiveness of Burgundy's description of the devastation caused by the war in France.

d The Chorus's reminder that after Henry's death his gains in France were lost and England suffered a civil war.

PART THREE

COMMENTARY

THEMES

PATRIOTISM

We are reminded several times in the play of previous English exploits in France. The Battle of Crécy, 1346, when the French were defeated by Edward III and his son, the Black Prince, is mentioned by the Archbishop of Canterbury in Act I, Scene 2, and by King Charles in Act II, Scene 4. The rhetoric of the Chorus in his descriptions of the army's preparations for the expedition (Act II), and Henry's speeches before Harfleur and Agincourt are calculated to rouse patriotic feelings in the audience.

There are a number of ways in which the English are shown to advantage and presented as being superior to their enemies. The unity and fellowship among the English is contrasted with the discord among the French. The French are shown as vain and incompetent, defeated by a small, sickly English army. At one point Henry boasts that one Englishman is worth three Frenchmen. Shakespeare shows the English as being civilised in their sparing of Harfleur, when in reality, the town was sacked. In the play we are presented with the view that God is on the side of the English.

KINGSHIP

As mentioned in the section on Henry's character, we are presented with the ideal of kingship in Henry V. Piety, humility, learning, courage, leadership, restraint and mercy are all demonstrated in this 'mirror of all Christian kings' (Act II, Chorus). Perhaps Shakespeare

intended Henry to be a flattering parallel for Queen
Elizabeth. He was certainly aware of the need for unity
and stability in his own time and would promote those
qualities which he thought would maintain the security
of the state. Henry does not recklessly attack France.
He secures England first by dealing with traitors at
home and by making provision against a Scottish
attack.

WARFARE

In the Chorus's description of the preparations for
invasion, at the beginning of Act II, we are given some
idea of the excitement generated by the prospects of the
glory and honour to be won in battle. Before Agincourt
Henry tells his troops that they will be respected and
envied for the rest of their lives if they survive. Even if
they die, their names will live for ever. However, in
addition to the rhetoric (see Literary Terms), and the
glories of the English victory we are given indications
of the darker aspects of war.

We also see that it attracts criminals and parasites, like
Pistol, Bardolph and Nym, who only go to steal. As
Pistol says, 'Let us to France, like horse-leeches, my
boys, To suck, to suck, the very blood to suck!' (Act II,
Scene 3).

Henry's speech to the Governor of Harfleur (Act III,
Scene 3), gives some indication of the horrors involved
in the sack of a town.

The night before Agincourt, Williams talks about the
hardships suffered by the families of poor soldiers.
Their wives and children may be left to starve if they
are killed. They have no choice but to obey the King
and it is suggested that the King bears a heavy
responsibility for waging war. After Agincourt, Exeter
gives an account of the bloody deaths of Suffolk and

York (Act IV, Scene 6) and Burgundy, in Act V, Scene 2, describes the devastation caused by the war in France and regrets the abandonment of the peaceful pursuits of the arts and learning.

These negative views of war add depth and credibility to the drama but do not significantly detract from its main thrust which is towards a patriotic celebration of the English triumph.

Love and friendship

One of the merits of the English side is the friendship between the leaders. Henry has affectionate words for Sir Thomas Erpingham and refers to him as 'old heart' (Act IV, Scene 1). Bedford and Exeter bid Salisbury a fond farewell before Agincourt, and we hear how, in the battle, the Duke of York kissed his dead friend Suffolk and died alongside him.

Henry extends his friendship to include all his soldiers and there is a general feeling of good fellowship in the English army.

The love between Henry and Katherine is not altogether convincing. Henry does tell Katherine he loves her, but he is clearly not about to die of it. Katherine agrees to marry him, but in reality she does not have much choice. Even though both Henry and Katherine try to make a good impression on the other, nothing can hide the fact that theirs is, first and foremost, a political union.

Structure

The structure and the unity of the play depend very much on the character of Henry as we see him exemplify the qualities of the ideal king. There are a number of events on the way to the achievement of his goals which do not, in themselves, form a strong plot. These are:

- Discussion and justification of the war
- Preparation and the suppression of treason
- Campaigning and setback in France
- Victory at Agincourt
- A satisfactory treaty and marriage agreement.

However, Shakespeare manages to create a drama around these events using the device of the Chorus who highlights their significance by:

- Filling in historical information, sometimes covering a span of several years
- Anticipating events so that the audience may have some knowledge not shared by characters, e.g. the exposure of the traitors
- Focusing our attention on the merits of Henry, 'This star of England' (Epilogue), and emphasising his central role in these great events

The comic sub-plots involving the low-life characters and Fluellen give the play some texture and light relief. The dishonesty and cowardice of some of these characters highlight the honesty and courage of Henry and his true followers. The low-life characters help to link this play with the others in the group and maintain a sense of historical continuity. The death of Falstaff can be seen as a signal that the days of Henry's youthful follies are truly dead and buried.

We are given regular views of the disunity and frivolity of the French leaders to emphasise the strength and harmony among the English:

- King Charles's hesitation and fear contrast with Henry's determination and decisive action

- Henry's sensible desire to avoid battle when he is in a weak position (Act III, Scene 6) is contrasted with the Dauphin's foolish, posturing threat to stab himself in defeat
- The friendship between Henry's nobles is set against the bickering and gossip of their French counterparts
- Henry's piety is contrasted with the frivolity of the French, their tempting of fate in their boasts and their casual use of oaths

CHARACTERS

KING HENRY

Henry dominates the play and completely overshadows the other characters. His words comprise about a third of the text.

Taken at face value it seems that Shakespeare has presented us with his view of the ideal monarch, 'the mirror of all Christian kings' (Act II, Chorus).

Henry is a devoutly religious man. We hear from the clergy that he is 'a true lover of the holy Church' (Act I, Scene 1) and that he is has a good knowledge of scripture and other areas of learning. He seeks the approval and support of the Church before waging war, and is aware of the horror and destruction which it brings. Henry prays sincerely, entrusting his enterprise to God's will and refusing to take credit for the victory at Agincourt, threatening with death any who boast of it and thus detract from God's achievement. He has paid for prayers and the building of chapels to compensate for his father's sins and after the battle he orders the singing of prayers and psalms in thanks to God. Unlike the French leaders, he does not use idle oaths or take God's name in vain.

Strong
Brave
Pious
Persuasive
Plain-spoken
Charismatic

Henry's physical courage is never in doubt. We see him leading his men at the siege of Harfleur and hear that he has been in personal combat at Agincourt.

As a leader of men Henry has wonderful insight. He encourages his nobles with references to their forefathers' deeds and flatters his men that he sees noble qualities in them. He reinforces their loyalty with talk of brotherhood and friendship and he leads by example. He refuses to arrange a ransom for himself. The Chorus tells us that the night before Agincourt he went around the English camp, inspiring his soldiers with confidence by his friendly words and cheerful manner. We can see that he takes his responsibilities seriously when he talks to Williams and the other common soldiers and later, in his only **soliloquy** (see Literary Terms), in which he talks of the heavy burden of kingship.

He is a skilful military commander and avoids useless loss of life. At Harfleur his eloquent warning to the Governor persuades him to surrender the town.

In matters of state Henry is firm and decisive. His reply to the Dauphin's tennis balls' insult is angry but dignified and restrained. He listens to the advice of others and considers such practical issues as the danger of a Scottish attack. He demands prompt replies from the French and will not be diverted from his goal. We see evidence of this on several occasions.

He dispenses justice in a fair and impartial manner. The three traitors are condemned because they have threatened the safety of the kingdom. He does not seek personal revenge and he can be magnanimous, as when he orders the release of the drunk who has shouted insults about him.

Henry has qualities which encourage us to believe in him as a human being, not just a paragon of kingly virtues. He has a sense of humour as demonstrated in the trick he plays on Fluellen and Williams. He is awkward and blunt when speaking to Katherine and is unable to court her with conventional flowery phrases and compliments. In his **soliloquy** in Act IV, Scene 1, he reveals his feelings about the responsibilities of kingship and the emptiness of ceremony and adulation.

It is possible to take a more negative view of Henry and some critics have described him as a cynical, ruthless manipulator. His piety can be viewed as a front which masks his ambition. It could be argued that he is merely setting up potential scapegoats, or seeking to spread the blame should he fail, when he enlists the support of the Church.

We may think him cold-hearted as he has turned his back on his old drinking companions. We hear complaints that he has broken Falstaff's heart and he is unmoved by the report of Bardolph's execution. If we look back to *Henry IV, Part 1*, the young Prince Hal made it clear that he was using Falstaff and his companions and would cast them off when the time came to show himself in a better light (*Henry IV, Part 1*, Act I, Scene 2).

However there is no real evidence to support the view that King Henry is wilfully deceiving people about his motives and his piety. He is as sincere when speaking in **soliloquy** as he is in public, and it is accepted that Shakespeare's characters reveal their true thoughts when speaking alone. Finally, the Chorus, who we may think of as expressing the views of the author, is always positive about Henry and full of praise for 'This star of England' (Epilogue).

PISTOL

One of the old low-life companions of Henry's youth, Pistol goes to France to profit from the war by thieving. He is a braggart and a coward who receives his just deserts at the hands of Fluellen. He speaks in a bombastic and ridiculous **parody** of **epic** verse full of **alliteration** (see Literary Terms) and windy nonsense. He provides much of the humour in the play through his speech, his cowardly behaviour and his encounters with Fluellen. However our sympathy towards him is limited by his attempts to lead the Boy into a life of crime and by his determination to continue in his dishonesty and to lie about his war exploits.

BARDOLPH

Bardolph, another of the low-life companions, is notable for his red nose, apparently the result of drinking. He is hanged for stealing from a church which causes a dispute between Pistol and Fluellen.

NYM

Nym is the third member of this gang. We first see him in a comic episode when he and Pistol threaten to fight each other, but both are too cowardly to do any harm. He does not say much but has a few catch-phrases such as, 'that's the humour of it'. He, too, is hanged for stealing.

THE BOY

The Boy is an unwilling party to the thieves' schemes. He goes to France as their servant after his master, Falstaff, dies. He gives us sharp and perceptive descriptions of these rogues and he plans to leave their company as soon as possible. He does not wish to follow them in a life of crime. The fact that they have attempted to corrupt this youth affects the audience's attitude to them. Sadly, we must assume that the Boy is killed when the French attack the baggage train in Act IV.

FLUELLEN

Professional
Serious
Conscientious
Talkative
Loyal
Proud

The Welsh captain is a serious-minded professional soldier. His version of the English language provides some simple humour. He tends to pronounce 'b' as 'p' and this produces some comic effects such as when he speaks of 'Alexander the pig' (Act IV, Scene 7), when he means Alexander the big, or great. He is also comical when he tries to hold discussions on the theory of warfare in the midst of battle, referring to the classical authors. His peculiar English, combined with his use of learned expressions result in some very amusing passages.

He is a brave soldier and despises cowards like Pistol. He is hot-headed and quick to take offence. He is particularly proud of his nationality and takes great delight in King Henry's acknowledgement of his own Welsh connections. He makes Pistol eat a leek for insulting the Welsh emblem on St David's day.

GOWER

The English captain is an honest even-tempered soldier. He seems to have the respect of the other captains and acts as a straight man to Fluellen in a number of comic situations. He tries to keep the peace between Fluellen and Macmorris, he recognises Pistol as a rogue when Fluellen has been fooled by the coward's boasts at the bridge and he approves of Fluellen's punishment of him in Act V, Scene 1.

MACMORRIS AND JAMY

These two captains appear only in Act II, Scene 2. Macmorris, the Irish captain, is quick-tempered and proud. He is a great believer in mines and gunpowder and he quarrels with Fluellen.

Jamy, the Scottish captain, is thoughtful and seems willing to discuss theory with Fluellen. Both captains speak in a comic version of their regional dialects.

The inclusion of English, Irish, Scots and Welsh captains may suggest that the whole of Britain is united against the French or that the English King had a right to rule over these countries. In fact, England and Scotland were not united until 1603 when King James came to the throne. He was already King James VI of Scotland, and became King James I of England.

THE ENGLISH SOLDIERS

Bates, Court and Williams are three common soldiers who Henry visits in disguise the night before Agincourt. They are thoughtful, plain-spoken men. They know they have most to lose in battle as they are too poor to be worth capturing for ransom and if they are killed their families will be destitute. Williams is the most outspoken of the three and eventually quarrels with Henry. After the battle when Henry reveals his identity, he still speaks up for himself and excuses himself in a dignified way. We do not see any French noble speaking to a common soldier and we hear references to mercenary troops in their army.

THE TRAITORS

Cambridge, Scroop and Grey all express remorse and accept their punishment when they are exposed. This is not a particularly convincing episode. It seems that they

are so dazzled by Henry's perfection that they are glad
to be caught. We are told that Scroop's treachery is
particularly wicked because he had been a close and
trusted companion of the King.

THE CHURCHMEN

The Archbishop of Canterbury and the Bishop of Ely
are two schemers who are concerned with protecting
the property and assets of the Church. It seems that
they are happy to encourage Henry to invade France
and will even finance the venture as it will keep him
from introducing the proposed heavy taxation of
Church property. They go beyond their remit of
providing legal advice when they actively encourage
Henry to attack France with reminders of previous
English victories.

EXETER

The Duke of Exeter, Henry's uncle, is a staunch and
loyal supporter of the young King. He arrests the
traitors in Act II, Scene 2, and he delivers the King's
demands to the French court in a very bold and
forthright way in Act II, Scene 4. Henry regards him as
being utterly reliable and leaves him in charge of
Harfleur (Act III, Scene 3), after it has been captured.
We hear of his bravery at the bridge from Fluellen in
Act III, Scene 6. He is foremost among those who
Henry delegates to settle the treaty in Act V, Scene 2,
while he courts Katherine.

KING CHARLES OF FRANCE

Weak

Indecisive

Cautious

Fearful

The French King is cautious and indecisive. He asks for
time to consider Henry's demands in Act II, Scene 4,
and again in Act V, Scene 2. He does not seem at all

confident in the face of the English threat and refers
to previous French defeats at the hands of Edward III.
He eventually gives in to all of Henry's demands.

PRINCESS KATHERINE

Katherine is a lively, intelligent girl. She would have
been fourteen at the time of Agincourt and eighteen
when she became engaged to Henry. We see her
sense of fun when she is attempting to learn English
in Act III, Scene 4. She provides light relief in this
scene between the serious events of the war. In the
final scene she shows that she is loyal to her country
when she questions whether she could love the enemy
of France. She is an obedient daughter as she gives
her consent to marry Henry only if her father wishes
it.

THE DAUPHIN

The Dauphin is vain and overconfident. He dismisses
Henry as a mere playboy and sends him the insult of
the tennis balls. He boasts about his horse and about
what he will do in the battle. However, he is almost
comical when he suggests stabbing himself when the
French are losing the fight. We are unsure about his
position as a leader. At first King Charles does not
allow him to go with the army, and he does not enjoy
the confidence of the other French leaders, particularly
the Constable of France.

THE CONSTABLE OF FRANCE

The Constable of France is a voice of reason among the
French. He cautions them against dismissing Henry as
an idle youth. He expresses a poor opinion of the
Dauphin's courage before the battle and admits to a

grudging sympathy for Henry, 'Alas, poor Harry of
England! He longs not for the dawning as we do.'
(Act III, Scene 7).

MONTJOY, THE HERALD

Henry respects Montjoy for his courage and for the
dignified and loyal way he carries out his duties,
whether he is delivering a message of defiance from the
French King or asking permission to gather the bodies
of the dead after the defeat.

LANGUAGE & STYLE

Two main types of speech are used in the play:
* **blank verse** (see Literary Terms)
* **prose** (see Literary Terms).

The noble and upper-class characters speak in **blank
verse**, but occasionally may speak in **prose** if the subject
matter is not important or if they are speaking to low-
class characters. The French nobles speak in prose in
Act II, Scene 7, as they are idly boasting and gossiping.
King Henry speaks in prose when he is in disguise and
talking to the soldiers. He also uses prose when he is
talking to Katherine, but this is to emphasise that he is
a plain-spoken soldier and lacks fancy words with
which to court her.

The verse is usually in lines of ten syllables. These are
called **iambic pentameters** (see Literary Terms) and are
based on a pattern of five pairs of syllables, each pair
consisting of an unstressed followed by a stressed
syllable. An example of this verse is

> 'For he today that sheds his blood with me
> Shall be my brother; be he ne'er so vile,' (Act IV, Scene 3).

Shakespeare does not stick rigidly to this pattern as it would become obvious and monotonous.

Prose is what we would consider everyday speech. This can vary a great deal. When Henry, in disguise, is speaking to the soldiers, he speaks in prose but it is rich and well-structured. Fluellen speaks in a comic version of Welsh-English, using stock phrases like, 'look you'. His speech is further affected by his choice of vocabulary and his wish to discuss military theory.

Macmorris and Davy also speak in comic versions of their dialects.

Among the lower-class characters, Pistol is the only one who speaks in verse, but it is a parody, or **mock-heroic** (see Literary Terms) type of verse. It is part of his boastful, bombastic pretence at bravery and is full of **alliteration** (see Literary Terms) and ridiculous theatrical phrases, e.g.

'O braggart vile and damned furious wight
The grave doth gape, and doting death is near;' (Act II, Scene 1).

In speeches like this Shakespeare was probably making fun of the style used by some other playwrights.

In the Chorus and in some of Henry's speeches there are elements of **rhetoric** (see Literary Terms), repetition of words or phrases, the building up of lists or questions and the balancing of phrases, for example,

'We few, we happy few, we band of brothers.' (Act IV, Scene 3)

'Show men dutiful?
Why, so didst thou. Seem they grave and learned?
Why, so didst thou. Came they of noble family?
Why, so didst thou. Seem they religious?
Why, so didst thou.' (Act II, Scene 2)

'Like little body with a mighty heart,' (Act II, Chorus)

A number of recurring **images** (see Literary Terms) and words are used in the play. We find words to do with speedy movement and flying, for example 'our wings' (Act I, Scene 2), 'winged heels, as English mercuries' (Act II, Chorus), 'winged thoughts' (Act V, Chorus).

The fierceness of the English soldiers is suggested by comparisons with wild animals, 'they will eat like wolves and fight like devils' (Act III, Scene 7), and hunting dogs, 'I see you stand like greyhounds in the slips, / Straining upon the start.' (Act III, Scene 1). At Harfleur, Henry encourages them to imitate the action of the tiger' (Act III, Scene 1).

Violence is also suggested by images of storms and other violent natural events such as whirlpools and earthquakes, for example,

> 'His approaches makes as fierce
> As waters to the sucking of a gulf.'   (Act II, Scene 4)

> 'Therefore in fierce Tempest is he coming
> In thunder and in earthquake, like a Jove,'
>
>   (Act II, Scene 4)

and

> 'Let the brow o'erwhelm it
> As fearfully as doth a galled rock
> O'erhang and jutty his confounded base,
> Swilled with the wild and wasteful ocean.'
>
>   (Act III, Scene 1).

PART FOUR

STUDY SKILLS

HOW TO USE QUOTATIONS

One of the secrets of success in writing essays is the way you use quotations. There are five basic principles:
- Put inverted commas at the beginning and end of the quotation
- Write the quotation exactly as it appears in the original
- Do not use a quotation that repeats what you have just written
- Use the quotation so that it fits into your sentence
- Keep the quotation as short as possible

Quotations should be used to develop the line of thought in your essays.

Your comment should not duplicate what is in your quotation. For example:

> **Fluellen refuses to intercede on behalf of Bardolph, and would be happy to see his own brother hanged in such circumstances because he believes in discipline. 'For if, look you, he were my brother, I would desire the Duke to use his good pleasure and put him to execution; for discipline ought to be used.' (Act III, Scene 6, lines 53–55)**

Far more effective is to write:

> **Fluellen says he will not help Bardolph. If he were his own brother he would, 'desire the Duke to use his good pleasure and put him to execution; for discipline ought to be used'.**

However, the most sophisticated way of using the writer's words is to embed them into your sentence:

> **Fluellen says that if Bardolph were his own brother he would wish the Duke to, 'put him to execution', because he believes, 'discipline ought to be used'.**

When you use quotations in this way, you are demonstrating the ability to use text as evidence to support your ideas - not simply including words from the original to prove you have read it.

Everyone writes differently. Work through the suggestions given here and adapt the advice to suit your own style and interests. This will improve your essay-writing skills and allow your personal voice to emerge.

The following points indicate in ascending order the skills of essay writing:
- Picking out one or two facts about the story and adding the odd detail
- Writing about the text by retelling the story
- Retelling the story and adding a quotation here and there
- Organising an answer which explains what is happening in the text and giving quotations to support what you write

....

- Writing in such a way as to show that you have thought about the intentions of the writer of the text and that you understand the techniques used
- Writing at some length, giving your viewpoint on the text and commenting by picking out details to support your views
- Looking at the text as a work of art, demonstrating clear critical judgement and explaining to the reader of your essay how the enjoyment of the text is assisted by literary devices, linguistic effects and psychological insights; showing how the text relates to the time when it was written

The dotted line above represents the division between lower and higher level grades. Higher-level performance begins when you start to consider your response as a reader of the text. The highest level is reached when you offer an enthusiastic personal response and show how this piece of literature is a product of its time.

Coursework essay

Set aside an hour or so at the start of your work to plan what you have to do.

- List all the points you feel are needed to cover the task. Collect page references of information and quotations that will support what you have to say. A helpful tool is the highlighter pen: this saves painstaking copying and enables you to target precisely what you want to use.
- Focus on what you consider to be the main points of the essay. Try to sum up your argument in a single sentence, which could be the closing sentence of your essay. Depending on the essay title, it could be a statement about a character: Just as Henry represents the ideal of kingship, Williams is the ideal of the ordinary plain-spoken Englishman; an opinion about setting: The French court is a place of weakness, indecision and disunity; or a judgement on a theme: The play, *Henry V*, is a treatise on the qualities of the ideal monarch.
- Make a short essay plan. Use the first paragraph to introduce the argument you wish to make. In the following paragraphs develop this argument with details, examples and other possible points of view. Sum up your argument in the last paragraph. Check you have answered the question.
- Write the essay, remembering all the time the central point you are making.
- On completion, go back over what you have written to eliminate careless errors and improve expression. Read it aloud to yourself, or, if you are feeling more confident, to a relative or friend.

If you can, try to type your essay, using a word processor. This will allow you to correct and improve your writing without spoiling its appearance.

Examination essay

The essay written in an examination often carries more marks than the coursework essay even though it is written under considerable time pressure.

In the revision period build up notes on various aspects of the text you are using. Fortunately, in acquiring this set of York Notes on *Henry V*, you have made a prudent beginning! York Notes are set out to give you vital information and help you to construct your personal overview of the text.

Make notes with appropriate quotations about the key issues of the set text. Go into the examination knowing your text and having a clear set of opinions about it.

In most English Literature examinations you can take in copies of your set books. This in an enormous advantage although it may lull you into a false sense of security. Beware! There is simply not enough time in an examination to read the book from scratch.

In the examination

- Read the question paper carefully and remind yourself what you have to do.
- Look at the questions on your set texts to select the one that most interests you and mentally work out the points you wish to stress.
- Remind yourself of the time available and how you are going to use it.
- Briefly map out a short plan in note form that will keep your writing on track and illustrate the key argument you want to make.
- Then set about writing it.
- When you have finished, check through to eliminate errors.

To summarise, these are the keys to success:

- **Know the text**
- **Have a clear understanding of and opinions on the storyline, characters, setting, themes and writer's concerns**
- **Select the right material**
- **Plan and write a clear response, continually bearing the question in mind**

A typical essay question on *Henry V* is followed by a sample essay plan in note form. This does not present the only answer to the question, merely one answer. Do not be afraid to include your own ideas and leave out some of those in the sample. Remember that quotations or close references to the text are essential to prove and illustrate the points you make.

How does Shakespeare seek to make us respond to Henry as a man?

Look through the play for occasions when Henry displays what you would consider to be human qualities as opposed to purely kingly virtues.

Part 1 Refer to the question. We have many examples of his kingly qualities. Name them. Perhaps give brief examples.

Part 2 Describe occasions where Henry shows affection and generosity
- release of the drunkard who insulted him
- towards Sir Thomas Erpingham
- friendly greetings to other nobles
- his generosity towards Montjoy
- generosity towards the Duke of York

Part 3 Describe Henry's relationships with the lower-class characters
- his approval of and relationship with Fluellen
- his talk with Williams and the others

Part 4 Discuss Henry's **soliloquy** (see Literary Terms) where he thinks about the burden of his responsibilities.

Part 5 Consider Henry's sense of humour, the joke he plays on Fluellen and Williams. Perhaps this is cruel or merely some light relief after the strain he has been under.

Part 6   Modesty and openness
                    • he is quite frank about his weak position when
                      speaking to Montjoy
                    • allows the Duke of York to take the most honoured
                      command in the battle
                    • makes no attempt at courtliness with Katherine

Conclusion   Consider the above qualities and examples and consider
                    how far they show Henry to be a sympathetic and
                    credible human being.

Further questions

Make a plan as shown opposite and attempt these
questions.

1 To what extent is Henry, 'the mirror of all Christian kings'?
2 What are the functions of the Chorus and how
   effective is he?
3 Discuss the ways in which Henry inspires his men
   before Harfleur and before Agincourt.
4 Compare and contrast the French court and nobles
   with the English.
5 Shakespeare creates humour through characters,
   situations and language. Discuss this with reference
   to one humorous scene.
6 How does Shakespeare create the impression of
   large-scale battles on his small stage?
7 Does *Henry V* present a narrow and nationalistic
   view of history that has little to offer today's
   audience?
8 Is Henry's religious devotion and piety convincing?
9 Does the glorification of war overshadow the
   reminders of its horrors in the play?
10 Is Fluellen a figure of fun, a hero, or both?

PART FIVE

CULTURAL CONNECTIONS

BROADER PERSPECTIVES

Films

There are two interesting and quite different film versions of the play.

Laurence Olivier's version (1945) was released in wartime and its patriotic message seemed very appropriate. It is set partly in a representation of Shakespeare's theatre and partly on location. Olivier gives a very powerful performance in the role of Henry.

Kenneth Branagh's production (1989) attempts greater realism in the battle scenes and focuses more on Henry's inner conflicts. There is not as much emphasis on the patriotic elements of the play as in Olivier's version. Branagh himself gives an excellent performance in the lead.

Chimes at Midnight (Orson Welles) is a wonderful compendium of *Henry IV, Part 1* and *Part 2*. It covers the events of Henry V's youth and his association with Falstaff and the other rogues. Orson Welles is brilliant as Falstaff. The film is particularly helpful in understanding the background to *Henry V*.

Plays

It would be helpful to see performances of any of the preceding plays in the group: *Richard II, Henry IV, Part 1* and *Henry IV, Part 2*.

Books

An A.B.C. of Shakespeare, Peter Bayley (Longman York Handbooks), is a useful resource.

The Face of Battle, John Keegan (Pimlico), a study of several battles, contains some interesting material about Agincourt.

Visiting a castle of the period may help to give you some idea of the problems faced by Henry at the siege of Harfleur.

Look at recruiting posters and other propaganda from the First World War and compare the sentiments with those expressed in Henry's rallying speeches and in the Chorus's speech at the beginning of Act II.

Some First World War poets wrote positive and patriotic poems, especially at the beginning of the war. In particular, look at 'For the Fallen' by Laurence Binyon and 'The Soldier' by Rupert Brooke. There are echoes of some of Henry's speeches in both. Compare the latter with Henry's speech to Montjoy in Act IV, Scene 3, where he says that the bodies of the English soldiers will continue to fight by rotting in the ground and causing a plague in France.

alliteration a series of similar consonant sounds, usually at the beginnings of words, to give rhythm or emphasis to a passage

blank verse lines which have a rhythmical pattern but do not rhyme. Most of this play is in blank verse, with iambic pentameters as the type of verse used

epic a long narrative poem dealing with a great hero, or a work or story on a similar theme

iambic pentameter a line of verse with five pairs of syllables, each pair consisting of an unstressed and a stressed syllable

image/imagery a picture in words either comparing one thing with another or giving it the qualities of another

mock-heroic treating a trivial subject with ridiculous, comic grandeur. Most of Pistol's speech is mock-heroic

parody an imitation which ridicules the original

patronage support of an artist by a wealthy person

prose ordinary spoken or written language, without set pattern or regular rhythm

pun a play on words; using a word that has two very different meanings. The Elizabethans were fond of puns and considered that someone who could pun well was intelligent

rhetoric the art of persuasive speaking. During the Middle Ages it was an essential subject of study

soliloquy a speech made by a character directly to the audience which reveals his or her thoughts

TEST YOURSELF (Act I)
A 1 Archbishop of Canterbury *(I.1.7–8)*
••• 2 King Henry *(I.2.96)*
3 Bishop of Ely *(I.2.115–6)*
4 French Ambassador *(I.2.252–3)*
5 Duke of Exeter *(I.2.299)*
6 King Henry *(I.2.309)*
7 King Henry *(I.1.54–5)*
8 The Dauphin *(I.2.282–3)*

TEST YOURSELF (Act II)
A 1 Chorus *(II.0.8)*
••• 2 Pistol *(II.1.61–2)*
3 King Henry *(II.2.40–1)*
4 Scroop *(II.2.151–2)*
5 The Dauphin *(II.4.71–3)*
6 Scroop *(II.2.10 11)*
7 Falstaff *(II.2.9–10)*
8 King Henry *(II.4.28)*

TEST YOURSELF (Act III)
A 1 King Henry *(III.1.24–5)*
••• 2 The Boy *(III.2.12–13)*
3 Fluellen *(III.2.58–9)*
4 Pistol *(III.6.38–40)*
5 King Henry *(III.7.163–4)*

6 The Dauphin *(III.7.80–1)*
7 Bardolph *(III.2.32–3)*
8 King Henry *(III.5.54–5)*
9 Pistol *(III.6.60–1)*
10 The Dauphin *(III.7.92)*

TEST YOURSELF (Act IV)
A 1 Pistol *(IV.1.37–8)*
••• 2 Constable of France *(IV.2.18)*
3 Westmorland *(IV.3.16–18)*
4 King Henry *(IV.3.38–39)*
5 The Dauphin *(IV.5.7)*
6 Fluellen *(IV.7.1)*
7 Montjoy *(IV.7.80–2)*
8 King Henry *(IV.0.41–2)*
9 Pistol *(IV.4.67)*
10 Duke of York *(IV.6.4–5)*

TEST YOURSELF (Act V)
A 1 Pistol *(V.1.28)*
••• 2 Burgundy *(V.2.23–4)*
3 King Henry *(V.2.149–151)*
4 Queen of France *(V.2.353–4)*
5 King Henry *(V.2.367–8)*
6 Pistol *(V.1.14)*
7 Fluellen *(V.1.75–7)*
8 Princess Katherine *(V.2.342–3)*

GCSE and equivalent levels (£3.50 each)

Maya Angelou
I Know Why the Caged Bird Sings

Jane Austen
Pride and Prejudice

Harold Brighouse
Hobson's Choice

Charlotte Brontë
Jane Eyre

Emily Brontë
Wuthering Heights

Charles Dickens
David Copperfield

Charles Dickens
Great Expectations

Charles Dickens
Hard Times

George Eliot
Silas Marner

William Golding
Lord of the Flies

Willis Hall
The Long and the Short and the Tall

Thomas Hardy
Far from the Madding Crowd

Thomas Hardy
The Mayor of Casterbridge

Thomas Hardy
Tess of the d'Urbervilles

L.P. Hartley
The Go-Between

Seamus Heaney
Selected Poems

Susan Hill
I'm the King of the Castle

Barry Hines
A Kestrel for a Knave

Louise Lawrence
Children of the Dust

Harper Lee
To Kill a Mockingbird

Laurie Lee
Cider with Rosie

Arthur Miller
A View from the Bridge

Arthur Miller
The Crucible

Robert O'Brien
Z for Zachariah

George Orwell
Animal Farm

J.B. Priestley
An Inspector Calls

Willy Russell
Educating Rita

Willy Russell
Our Day Out

J.D. Salinger
The Catcher in the Rye

William Shakespeare
Henry V

William Shakespeare
Julius Caesar

William Shakespeare
Macbeth

William Shakespeare
A Midsummer Night's Dream

William Shakespeare
The Merchant of Venice

William Shakespeare
Romeo and Juliet

William Shakespeare
The Tempest

William Shakespeare
Twelfth Night

George Bernard Shaw
Pygmalion

R.C. Sherriff
Journey's End

Rukshana Smith
Salt on the snow

John Steinbeck
Of Mice and Men

R.L. Stevenson
Dr Jekyll and Mr Hyde

Robert Swindells
Daz 4 Zoe

Mildred D. Taylor
Roll of Thunder, Hear My Cry

Mark Twain
The Adventures of Huckleberry Finn

James Watson
Talking in Whispers

A Choice of Poets

Nineteenth Century Short Stories

Poetry of the First World War

Six Women Poets

Advanced level (£3.99 each)

Margaret Atwood
The Handmaid's Tale

William Blake
Songs of Innocence and of Experience

Emily Brontë
Wuthering Heights

Geoffrey Chaucer
The Wife of Bath's Prologue and Tale

Joseph Conrad
Heart of Darkness

Charles Dickens
Great Expectations

F. Scott Fitzgerald
The Great Gatsby

Thomas Hardy
Tess of the d'Urbervilles

James Joyce
Dubliners

Arthur Miller
Death of a Salesman

William Shakespeare
Antony and Cleopatra

William Shakespeare
Hamlet

William Shakespeare
King Lear

William Shakespeare
The Merchant of Venice

William Shakespeare
Romeo and Juliet

William Shakespeare
The Tempest

Mary Shelley
Frankenstein

Alice Walker
The Color Purple

Tennessee Williams
A Streetcar Named Desire